EYE TO EYE WITH DOGS

GERMAN SHEPHERDS

Lynn M. Stone

Rourke
Publishing LLC
Vero Beach, Florida 32964

PHOTO CREDITS: All photos © Lynn M. Stone

Cover: *Today's German Shepherds were bred from a variety of shepherd dogs in Germany in the late 1800s.*

Acknowledgments: For their help in the preparation of this book, the author thanks humans Craig Bahe, June Connelly, Terri Lappin, and Jonathan Peck; and canines Ike, Nero, and others

Editor: Frank Sloan

Cover and page design by Nicola Stratford

Library of Congress Cataloging-in-Publication Data

Stone, Lynn M.
    German shepherds / Lynn M. Stone
        p. cm. — (Eye to eye with dogs)
    Summary: A brief introduction to the physical characteristics, temperament, uses, and breeding history of the German shepherd dog.
    Includes bibliographical references (p.).
    ISBN 1-58952-327-X
    1. German shepherd dog—Juvenile literature. [1. German shepherd dog. 2. Dogs.] I. Title

SF429.G37 S75 2002
636.737'6—dc21   2002017842

Printed in the USA

MP/W

Table of Contents

German shepherds are large, handsome dogs with athletic builds.

The German Shepherd

A few kinds of dogs can be taught to do amazing things. Those dogs almost seem part human! They are not, of course, but they seem too bright to be, well, just dogs.

One of the most remarkable dog **breeds** is the German shepherd. German shepherds are big, handsome, athletic dogs.

GERMAN SHEPHERD FACTS	
Weight:	75-95 pounds (34-43 kilograms)
Height:	22-26 inches (55-66 centimeters)
Country of Origin:	Germany
Life Span:	12-13 years

Most German shepherds live as home and family companions. But some of them work as guide, or seeing-eye, dogs. Others are police dogs and guard dogs.

Many German shepherds are used as police dogs in North America, like Ike in this photo.

Most German shepherds are kept as family companions, not as working dogs.

Some are used to sniff out drugs, explosives, or lost or injured people. Some are trained for **obedience** trials. A few are still used as herd dogs, or shepherds.

Special Abilities

German shepherds have a long list of abilities. Those abilities are among the reasons for the dogs' great popularity. They are the third most popular **purebred** dog in both the United States and Canada.

Their popularity had a boost many years ago from television and movies. Both Strongheart and Rin Tin Tin were German shepherds.

Once the most popular purebred dog in North America, German shepherds are now number three.

The wolf is the ancestor of all dogs.

German shepherds were once called Alsatian wolfdogs in Great Britain. German shepherds do look more wolf-like than most dogs. But the "wolfdog" name frightened people, so it was dropped.

Are German shepherds closely related to wolves? The wolf was the common **ancestor** of all dogs. But German shepherds are no more or less closely related to wolves than other dogs.

German Shepherds of the Past

Many hundreds of years ago, wolf-like dogs were known in the area that would become Germany. They weren't exactly German shepherds. However, they may have been among the shepherd's first dog ancestors.

The modern German shepherd is the result of work by German dog breeders in the late 1800s.

White German shepherds have been developed by breeders in recent times.

The modern German shepherd is the result of work by Max von Stephanitz and other German dog **breeders**. Their work began in the late 1800s. They used a variety of shepherd dogs from Germany to develop the modern German shepherd.

13

Those first German shepherds had three different types of coats: shorthaired, longhaired, and wirehaired. Dog clubs in most countries now show only shorthaired shepherds.

Early in the 1900s the breed spread rapidly from Germany to other countries.

German shepherds with short hair are by far the most popular type.

A German shepherd's size, sharp muzzle, and erect ears give it a wolfish look.

Looks

German shepherds have a "wolfish" look. They are large, like wolves, and they share similarly shaped heads. They also have pointed, upright ears like wolves. Most German shepherds are shorthaired. A few have long, silky hair.

German shepherds may be black and tan, black and gray, or all black. Some are cream-colored or white. (The American Kennel Club does not accept these light-colored dogs.)

German Shepherd Companions

Choosing a German shepherd for a pet is not easy. German shepherds come in many different personalities. Those bred by wise, careful breeders are usually wonderful dogs—handsome, brave, and obedient.

A well-bred German shepherd dog makes an excellent canine companion.

For better or worse, this German shepherd pup will likely have a personality much like its parents.

But like most popular purebred dogs, German shepherds may have problems if their parents aren't chosen carefully. Some German shepherds, for example, are overly nervous or even timid. Some are very **aggressive** toward other dogs.

Dog breeders in North America have generally chosen easy-going German shepherd dogs to be parents. Many North American German shepherds are good-natured and calm. German shepherds used for police work in North America are often imported from Germany. These dogs are usually more aggressive than their North American cousins.

The floppy ears of this German shepherd pup will stand straight as the dog grows up.

A Note About Dogs

Puppies are cute and cuddly, but buying one should never be done without serious thought. Choosing the right breed of dog requires some homework. And remember that a dog will require more than love and great patience. It will require food, exercise, grooming, a warm, safe place to live, and medical care.

A dog can be your best friend, but you need to be its best friend, too. For more information about buying and owning a dog, contact the American Kennel Club at http://www.akc.org/index.cfm or the Canadian Kennel Club at http://www.ckc.ca/.

Glossary

aggressive (uh GRES iv) — to act forcefully

ancestor (AN ses tur) — one in the past from whom an animal has descended; direct relative from the past

breeders (BREE duhrz) — people who raise animals, such as dogs, and carefully choose the mothers and fathers for more dogs

breeds (BREEDZ) — particular kinds of domestic animals within a larger group, such as the German shepherd breed within the dog group

obedience (oh BEE dee ehns) — the willingness to follow someone's direction or command

purebred (PYOOR bred) — an animal of a single (pure) breed

Index

Further Reading

Margolis, Matthew and Siegal, Mordecai. *The Good Shepherd: A Pet Owner's Guide to the German Shepherd, Vol. 1*. Little, Brown, 1996

Websites to Visit

German Shepherd Dogs at http://www.germanshepherds.com
German Shepherd Dogs at http://www.cluebus.com/holly/gsdfaq.html

About the Author

Lynn Stone is the author of over 400 children's books. He is a talented natural history photographer as well. Lynn, a former teacher, travels worldwide to photograph wildlife in its natural habitat.